Kingdom Files:

Who Was David?

Kingdom Files:

Who Was David?

Matt Koceich

BARBOUR BOOKS
An Imprint of Barbour Publishing, Inc.

Print ISBN 978-1-68322-628-4

eBook Editions:
Adobe Digital Edition (.epub) 978-1-68322-896-7
Kindle and MobiPocket Edition (.prc) 978-1-68322-902-5

Cover design by C. B. Canga
Interior illustration by Patricia Yuste

Published by Barbour Books, an imprint of Barbour Publishing, Inc., 1810
Barbour Drive, Uhrichsville, Ohio 44683, www.barbourbooks.com

Our mission is to inspire the world with the life-changing message of the Bible.

Member of the
Evangelical Christian
Publishers Association

Printed in the United States of America.

06136 0718 CM

Dear Reading Detective,

Welcome to Kingdom Files! You're now a very important part of the Kingdom Files investigation—a series of really cool biographies all found in the Bible. Each case you investigate focuses on an important Bible character and is separated into three sections to make your time fun and interesting. First, you'll find the **Fact File**, which contains key information about a specific Bible character whom God called to do big things for His kingdom. Next, you'll read through an **Action File** that lays out Bible events showing the character in action. And finally, the **Power File** is where you'll find valuable information and memory verses to help you see how God is working in your life too. Along the way, **Clue Boxes** will offer applications to help you keep track of your thoughts as you make your way through the files. You can also use these sections to record questions you might have along David's journey. Write down any questions, and then ask your parents to get them involved in your quest.

Before you begin, know this: not only did God have plans for the Bible characters you'll read about in the Kingdom Files, but Jeremiah 29:11 says that God has big plans for you too! I pray that *Kingdom Files: Who Was David?* helps you get a bigger picture of God, and that you will see just how much He loves you!

Blessings,
M.K.

Name: **DAVID**

Occupation: **king, mighty warrior, writer of psalms**

From: **Bethlehem**

Years Active: **1025–970 BC**

Kingdom Work: **king of Israel, fought for God's people, wrote songs**

Mini Timeline:

▲
1025 BC
Samuel anoints David as future king

▲
1020 BC
David kills Goliath

▲
993 BC
David reigns over all Israel and Judah

Key Stats:

+ Brought the people of Israel together

+ Helped the Israelites win battles and conquer land

+ Made it possible for his son Solomon to build the temple

CLUES

The temple was built in Jerusalem and was mainly used as the place to offer sacrifices to God. The most important part of the temple was called the holy of holies, and in it were the Ten Commandments and the ark of the covenant. Once a year, the high priest would go into the holy of holies, pray to God, and ask God to forgive the people of Israel's sins.

Early Life

To begin our investigation into the life of David, it helps to understand a few background notes first. David's story is found in the Old Testament books of 1 Samuel, 2 Samuel, 1 Kings, and 1 Chronicles. When David was young, a king named Saul had ruled over the land of Israel for forty-two years. He became selfish, so God decided to call a new young man to take the throne.

God sent his prophet, Samuel, to David's house. So Samuel went to Bethlehem where he found a man named Jesse, who was David's father. David was the youngest of eight sons. He worked as a shepherd tending his father's

flock. Jesse introduced his sons to Samuel,
but the prophet asked if there were any others.
That's when Jesse called for David, and imme-
diately Samuel knew this was who he was
supposed to anoint as king. The Bible says that
at this point, the Spirit of God came on David

with power (1 Samuel 16:13).

Meanwhile, King Saul was being attacked
by an evil spirit. He asked his servants to bring
someone who could play music to help calm his

nerves. The
servants knew
about David,
and so Jesse
sent his son
David to Saul
with a donkey
loaded with
bread and wine
and a young
goat as gifts for the king. Saul was so pleased with
David and his music playing that he had David
stay with him to be in his service.

At the same time, there was an army called
the Philistines who were close by, trying to

attack the Israelites. King Saul gathered the Israelites to fight and defend their towns (1 Samuel 17:2–3). When they went out to engage in battle, Saul and his men were confronted by a horrifying sight. There was one Philistine in particular named Goliath. The Bible says that Goliath was over nine feet tall and wore a bronze helmet and armor that

 CLUES

Even the giant's spear had a fifteen-pound iron point!

weighed 125 pounds!

The giant began taunting the king and his army. Goliath yelled out a challenge. He asked for a man who would be willing to fight him. He said that if he won, the Israelites would become slaves to the Philistines; and if one of Saul's men won, the Philistines would become servants to the Israelites. King Saul was terrified! (1 Samuel 17:11).

This exchange went on for forty days. Morning and night, Goliath approached the Israelites, asking for a man who would be willing to fight. No one dared fight the superhuman giant.

Meanwhile, David was in charge of taking food to his older brothers. They were a part of the Israelite army and within clear view of the giant. David ran out to the battle lines to check on his brothers and make sure they were okay. As soon as David saw Goliath, he wanted to know who

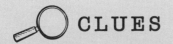

CLUES

David told Saul about how when lions or bears would come to capture the sheep, he would go after the predators and save the sheep from being eaten. He also added that if the animal tried to attack him, he was strong enough to take its life. David then compared Goliath to the wild animals: "The LORD who rescued me from the paw of the lion and the paw of the bear will rescue me from the hand of this Philistine" (1 Samuel 17:37).

he was. David was upset because of the way the giant didn't respect God (1 Samuel 17:26).

David's oldest brother was angry at him, because he thought David was only there to watch a good fight. Saul heard about David's courage and sent for him. In the king's chambers, David told Saul not to lose heart because of Goliath's threats. And then David offered to go and fight the giant!

Saul wasn't convinced. He thought David was too young and unable to win a battle with the giant. Saul added that Goliath had been a warrior for a very long time. But David was ready with a reply. He told Saul about his job tending sheep.

King Saul finally agreed to let David go and fight the giant. He began by putting his personal armor on David. But David couldn't move around in the heavy armor. David armed himself with only his staff and his sling, and he chose five stones from a nearby stream and put them in a pouch. Then he went out to meet Goliath.

The superhuman laughed. "Am I a dog, that you come at me with sticks? . . . Come here. . . and I'll give your flesh to the birds and the wild animals!" (1 Samuel 17:43–44). David knew that God was on his side and responded to the giant not with fear but with courage. "You come against me with sword and spear and javelin, but I come against you in the name of the LORD Almighty"

(1 Samuel 17:45). David said that he was confident that God would deliver the giant into his hands. And then he added that after he won the battle, the

whole world would know that God was in charge.

David also said that the battle belonged to God and that God would give not only Goliath, but all the Philistines, into the Israelites' hands. At that, the giant moved quickly to attack David. David didn't hesitate. He ran toward the giant. As he ran, David took a stone and slung it at Goliath. The stone hit the giant on the forehead, causing him to fall dead "facedown on the ground" (1 Samuel 17:49). At the sight of this unbelievable event, the Philistines took off running. David kept Goliath's weapons. King Saul was very impressed that David had taken care of the wicked giant and a very massive problem!

In the King's Service

Saul kept David with him instead of letting him return home to Bethlehem. A man named Jonathan, who was the king's eldest son, befriended David during this time. Saul sent David on many missions. David was very successful and was given a high rank in the king's army. All

the troops were grateful for David's promotion.

The Bible says that one day when David was playing music, an evil spirit came over Saul and he tried to throw a spear at David, but David

CLUES

Soon, the people were praising David more than they were praising King Saul—and this made the king angry. He kept a close watch on David to make sure he didn't take more attention from the king.

was quick to move out of the way. Saul soon became afraid of David. He put David in charge of a thousand men to lead into battles. David had success in everything he did because "the LORD was with him" (1 Samuel 18:14). The Israelite people continued to love David because of his great leadership.

Saul became very worried that David would take his throne, so he tried to trick the young man. He wanted David to marry his older daughter, but David didn't feel worthy, so the marriage never happened. But Saul wouldn't take no for an answer. He offered his other daughter's hand in marriage. Saul had his

attendants talk to David to try to convince him
to agree to the union. But again, David said he
wasn't worthy of marrying the king's daughter
because he was "a poor man and little known"
(1 Samuel 18:23).

Saul couldn't believe David's refusal, because
he wanted David to obey him. The king tried
sending David back out to battle, hoping that the
Philistines would take his life. But nothing went

the way Saul wanted it to go. David eventually married Saul's daughter, and Saul realized that the Lord was with David. The Bible says that Saul remained "his enemy the rest of his days" (1 Samuel 18:29).

CLUES

The king's plan continued to backfire. The more David battled the Philistines, the more success he had. As a result, David became more and more popular among the people. So Saul stopped trying to come up with different ways to hurt David. His new plan? He ordered his son Jonathan and all the servants to take David's life.

Since Jonathan was David's friend, he told him of his father's plan to take his life. Jonathan told David to hide and also said that he would talk to Saul in hopes of helping David. Jonathan told his father that David was a good person and that David hadn't done anything wrong. In fact, he said everything David had done actually helped Saul.

The king heard his son and came to his senses. He promised he wouldn't do anything to harm David.

But as time passed, once again Saul tried to harm David with a spear. And yet again, David was quicker and avoided getting hurt. After this incident, David escaped the castle. Saul was furious and sent men to David's house in Bethlehem, but David's wife Michal warned him of her father's plan. After David ran away, Michal  took a statue and put it in David's bed. She also covered the idol with some clothes and even put "goats' hair at the head" (1 Samuel 19:13).

The king sent men to capture David, but Michal intercepted them and said that David was sick. Saul wouldn't be defeated and sent his men again to bring David, sick or not, back to him. That's when the men found the statue instead of David. Saul asked his daughter why she had deceived him. She said that David threatened her, even though it had been her idea to help him escape.

Meanwhile, when David fled, he found Samuel and told him everything that had happened with Saul. Then the two of them went to a town called Naioth, about five miles northwest of Jerusalem. Not

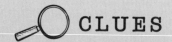 CLUES

A prophet was a person chosen by God to speak for Him. They would tell people about God and what He expected, and they would remind people to obey God and to worship Him with all their hearts. Saul's men were overcome by God's Spirit, and they too began praising God along with the prophets.

long after, the king learned where David was and sent men to capture him. The Bible says that when Saul's men arrived at the place where David was staying, they saw Samuel leading a group of prophets prophesying (1 Samuel 19:20).

Saul heard of this and sent more men, but like the first group, they also joined in with the others and began praising God. Saul sent a third group of men, and they also joined the others and praised God. Saul decided to go to find David himself!

When he arrived, the king asked where Samuel and David were and was told to go to Naioth. Then the Spirit came over Saul, and he walked along praising God on his way to find David. He found Samuel and kept prophesying all that day and all through the night. This wasn't what the king had in mind when he went after David. The people were so amazed they thought Saul was one of the prophets!

On the Run

David received word that Saul was after him, so he went back to find his friend Jonathan. Once the two friends were reunited, David asked why Jonathan's father was trying to take his life. Jonathan told David not to worry. He said that his father always told him his plans and that he hadn't heard about the horrible things David was saying.

David told Jonathan that Saul knew he and Jonathan were friends. Saul, in David's opinion, didn't want to see his son grieved by David's passing. But David believed that Saul would still find him and take his life. Jonathan replied, "Whatever you want me to do, I'll do it for you."

Jonathan vowed never to turn David over to his father.

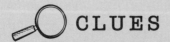

CLUES

David came up with a plan to test the king's heart. He told Jonathan that he was going to hide out in the field. He said that if Saul acted like he missed David, then Jonathan should say that David had gone back to Bethlehem to join his family in an annual sacrifice. David told his friend that if Saul was okay with that, then David knew he was safe. However, David knew that if Saul lost his temper over the story, then he would face extreme danger.

The two friends went out into the fields and came up with an idea. Jonathan told David to hide behind a big stone. He said he would shoot three arrows at it like he was taking target practice. Then when he sent a servant to retrieve the arrows, Jonathan would send David a code so he would know whether it was safe to stay or if he should run away.

The next day when Saul sat with his family for a feast, he noticed that David was absent. Saul

thought nothing of it, but when David was missing from the gathering for the second day's meal, the king asked his son Jonathan for an explanation. Jonathan protected David by telling Saul a story about David's family wanting him there for a sacrifice and that one of David's brothers had ordered him to be there in Bethlehem for it (1 Samuel 20:29).

Saul became infuriated with Jonathan's response because David got away. Saul was angry because he knew that Jonathan had helped David escape. Saul threatened his own son by saying,

CLUES

Jonathan knew that his father intended to kill David. This made Jonathan very sad. He couldn't eat and was very angry and ashamed at the way Saul wanted to mistreat David.

"As long as the son of Jesse lives on this earth, neither you nor your kingdom will be established" (1 Samuel 20:31). Then Saul ordered his son to have someone find David and bring him to the royal palace. Jonathan tried sticking up for his friend by asking Saul what David had done wrong.

The next morning, Jonathan went out to meet David in the fields. A small boy was with him to collect the arrows. Jonathan yelled out, "Isn't the arrow beyond you? . . . Hurry! Go quickly! Don't stop!" (1 Samuel 20:37–38). This, of course, was the friends' code, and the boy had no idea that David was close by and could hear Jonathan's secret message. When the boy returned the arrows, Jonathan told him to take them back to the village. After the boy left, David came out from his hiding place behind the stone and bowed before Jonathan.

Both men cried together because of the sad news that Saul had every intention of killing David. Finally, Jonathan told David to head out in peace and reminded him that they would be friends forever. Eventually, David left and Jonathan headed back to town.

The Bible says that David went to a town called Nob where he met the priest Ahimelek. The priest asked David why he was traveling alone. David replied by saying that the king had sent him on a secret mission and that his men were sent a different direction. David then asked the man for food.

While this was going on, the chief shepherd of Saul was there. David asked the priest if he had a weapon he could borrow. Ahimelek said the sword of Goliath was there. David agreed that it was a special sword, so he took it and fled from

Saul's servant. David went to the king of Gath, Achish. The Bible says that David was afraid of the king and pretended to be insane. David acted like a madman, "making marks on the doors of the gate and letting saliva run down his beard" (1 Samuel 21:13). Achish was enraged. He couldn't believe his servants would bring such a lunatic into his presence.

David took off from Gath and ran to the cave of Adullam. His family received word where David was, and they went to him there.

Soon nearly four hundred men—people who were unhappy, in debt, or stressed out—gathered with

David and "he became their commander" (1 Samuel 22:2).

David continued his escape journey and went to a place called Mizpah in the land of Moab. He found the king in Moab and asked if his parents could stay with him until he learned what God was going to do.

A prophet named Gad came to David and warned him to leave. "Do not stay. . . . Go into the land of Judah" (1 Samuel 22:5). Again, David ran away and headed into the forest of Hereth.

Saul received news that his men had discovered David's whereabouts. He sat holding a spear and addressed all his officials who were nearby. Saul started asking them questions about David's character and intentions. "Will the son of Jesse give all of you fields and vineyards? Will he make all of you commanders of thousands?" (1 Samuel 22:7).

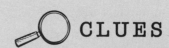

CLUES

Saul was mad because he wanted to know why his men weren't helping him capture David. Saul thought maybe they had made bargains with the fugitive.

One of the king's servants, Doeg the Edomite, spoke up and told Saul about how David went to the man named Ahimelek at Nob and how the man provided for David and even gave him Goliath's sword. This information made Saul angry. The king sent for Ahimelek and questioned him as to why he would help David. The man said

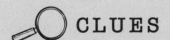

CLUES

Edom was a land that bordered Israel and is now southwest Jordan. It was a popular place because of its location on the trade route between Arabia and the Mediterranean Sea.

that he knew that David was the most loyal servant in all of Saul's army.

Saul ignored the truth and became enraged. He threatened to take the man's life and ordered his guards to take the lives of all the priests because Saul thought they too had helped David. Saul was in for a surprise, for his guards refused to obey him. Because they were God's priests, the guards didn't want to harm them.

Saul wouldn't be outdone. He turned to Doeg again and ordered him to strike down the priests. Unlike the guards, Doeg obeyed the command. As Doeg carried out the evil order, one man named Abiathar escaped and found David. He told David of the horrible attack on the priests. David had remorse because he had met Doeg before and had a feeling that he would tell Saul about David and how Ahimelek had helped him. And he felt like he was responsible for the horrible murders. David invited Abiathar to stay with him since they had a common enemy in Saul.

Still Running

A battle was raging near David's location in a place called Keilah. The Philistines were attacking the people and stealing their possessions. David asked God if he should go and attack the Philistines. God said yes and instructed David to save the city. David told his men about the plan, but they were afraid to go into battle against the Philistines. This made David go back to the Lord and ask what he should do. God said, "Go down to Keilah, for I am going to give the Philistines into your hand" (1 Samuel 23:4).

David took his men and went down to Keilah, and they were victorious over the Philistines, saving the people there. Yet again, Saul would not go away or be defeated by David. Saul received information that

David had gone to the town of Keilah.

But this time it was David who received information about Saul's intent to come and attack David. David went to God in prayer, asking if Saul was on his way to attack and if the people of Keilah

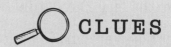 CLUES

The king was happy because he felt that David would be easy to capture since he had gone into a town with "gates and bars" (1 Samuel 23:7), meaning it was built up to protect the people who lived there. Saul gathered all his forces to help capture David and his men.

would turn David over to Saul. God answered yes to both questions.

David gathered his men, now totaling around six hundred, and took off in escape. They didn't stop but kept moving from place to place, trying to outwit Saul and his army. Saul was told of David's escape and decided not to go to Keilah. David stayed in the wilderness and in the hills trying to outrun Saul. Saul did try to hunt David down, but he failed because "God did

 CLUES

At this time, Jonathan, King Saul's son and David's friend, came back into David's life. He found David in Horesh and helped him reconnect with God. Jonathan reminded David to find all of his strength in God alone. He said, "Don't be afraid.... My father Saul will not lay a hand on you. You will be king over Israel.... Even my father Saul knows this" (1 Samuel 23:17). These words helped David know that God was on his side. Jonathan went home, and David remained in Horesh.

not give David into his hands" (1 Samuel 23:14).

Just like all the other times before, while David was being reminded that he was doing God's work, Saul was close on his heels. This time a group of people known as the Ziphites met Saul and told him that they knew exactly where David was hiding. They invited Saul to come down to where they were and offered to hand David over to him. Saul was excited and grateful that someone was willing to help him capture David. Saul told them to get more information, like places David normally went and who went to see him. The king knew David was clever, and he didn't want to lose

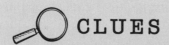

CLUES

David and his men were in a place called the Desert of Maon. As Saul and his people gave chase, David was warned about it, so he stayed in the desert. Saul got news of where David was hiding, so he headed to the desert too.

him. Saul wanted definite information about all the hiding places David used. Saul would then be armed with enough information to go after his prey.

In between Saul and David was a large mountain. David and his men were on one side and Saul and his guards were on the other. Saul was closing the gap. The chase was almost over. Just as Saul and his men were about to capture David, a messenger told Saul that the dreaded Philistines were raiding the land. When he received this news, Saul broke off from pursuing David and

went out to meet the Philistines.

After Saul left, David went and lived in a place called En Gedi. Saul came back from his

pursuit of the Philistines and began to look for David again. He was given information that David was staying in a place called the Crags of the Wild Goats. Saul took three thousand men and went

out in search of David. Along the way, Saul entered a cave, but what the king didn't know was that David and his men were in the back of the very same cave. David crept up and cut off a piece of Saul's robe.

David felt bad for what he had done, and he told his men that they were not allowed to attack Saul. They let him leave the cave untouched. After Saul left the cave, David walked out and called out to him, "My lord the king!" (1 Samuel 24:8). Saul turned, and David bowed down. He asked Saul why he had listened to the people who told him that David was trying to harm him. He went on to remind Saul that the Lord had delivered the king into David's hands. He said he had men who had urged him to take Saul's life,  but he refused. David told Saul that he would not harm him and showed him the piece of robe that he had cut off. David was using that as proof that he did not have any intention of harming Saul.

Saul began to cry because he realized that David had spared his life. Saul even asked God to reward David for the way he treated Saul. Saul asked David to promise that he wouldn't harm his family, and David promised. Eventually, Saul returned home, and David and his men returned to their hiding place.

The next part of David's journey took him to Maon, in the area of Carmel. A man named Nabal who was very wealthy lived there. Nabal's wife was Abigail. Nabal owned three thousand sheep, and David heard about him and sent men to him with a message. Nabal had shepherds who had spent time with David's group. David's men had helped protect their flocks. So David sent a message to Nabal in hopes of getting help with food and provisions.

When Nabal listened to David's men, he didn't respond kindly. He questioned who David was and asked why he should share his food with people he didn't know. When David's men returned to him with Nabal's reply, David told them to get their swords. About four hundred men went with David to confront Nabal.

One of Abigail's servants told her that Nabal had hurled insults at David's men earlier in the day. The servant confirmed that David's people had been very good to them and explained how David and his men had protected them while they were out in the fields with the sheep. The servant told Abigail that disaster was on its way because Nabal had dismissed David's plea for help.

Abigail came up with a plan. She gathered up "two hundred loaves of bread, two skins of wine, five dressed sheep, [sixty pounds] of roasted grain, a hundred cakes of raisins, and two hundred cakes of pressed figs" (1 Samuel 25:18). She had it loaded up on donkeys and told her servants to head toward David and his men and that she would follow behind. Abigail did not tell her husband what she was doing. As she rode her donkey, Abigail looked out and saw David and his men approaching in the distance.

Abigail got off her donkey and bowed before David. She asked permission to speak to David, and he listened. Abigail told David not to listen to anything Nabal said. She even told David that her husband's name meant "fool." Abigail let David know she hadn't seen the group of men he sent who had asked for help. Then she presented the generous food offering to David.

Abigail said that she believed God would be with David, because David fought the Lord's battles. She told him not to worry about being hunted by Saul, because she knew God would protect him. Abigail also told David that she believed he would become the ruler over Israel. She finally asked David to remember her.

When she arrived home, she found that Nabal was having a wild party with a lot of food and drink. The next morning, she told her husband all that had happened with David, and the Bible says Nabal's heart began to hurt. Several days later, Nabal passed away. After

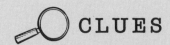 **CLUES**

David praised God for Abigail. He asked for her to be blessed because of her good judgment and the way her actions helped keep David from attacking Nabal and his men. David accepted Abigail's offering and sent her back home in peace.

word of Nabal's passing reached David, David sent a message back to Abigail asking for her hand in marriage. Abigail agreed and soon became David's wife.

5

So Close

Yet again, Saul went in search of David. The Ziphites told Saul that David was hiding in the hills of Hakilah. Saul gathered three thousand select troops to search for the runaway shepherd. He made a camp by the roadside, but David stayed in the wilderness. David sent scouts to watch Saul, and after a while he went to the place where Saul was. He found where Saul slept and saw his army surrounding him.

David asked his people who would go with him to Saul, and a man named Abishai volunteered. David and his friend went to Saul's camp and found the king sleeping with his spear on the ground nearby. Abishai told David that God had delivered Saul into his hands. He wanted to

be done with Saul, but David warned against bringing harm to the man, no matter how bad he was. David knew that God had anointed Saul, and so David wanted to respect that fact. David wanted to let God deal with Saul instead. David made sure they took Saul's spear and water jug before they left his tent.

David crossed over to the other side of the hill from Saul's camp.

 CLUES

No one knew or saw David and Abishai because the Lord had put Saul and his men into a deep sleep (1 Samuel 26:12).

He called out to one of Saul's men named Abner, who was in charge of guarding the king. When he answered, David asked Abner why he hadn't protected Saul. He told him that someone had come in the night to destroy Saul. David finished by asking Abner where the king's spear and water jug were.

Saul heard David's voice and called out to him. David asked Saul why he was trying to hunt him down. Saul responded, saying he had sinned and that he wouldn't bring harm to David. Saul also admitted to acting like a fool. David gave Saul back his spear. Saul said that he hoped David would be  blessed and that he knew David would go on to do great things. David went his way, and Saul went back to his home.

Even though David had gotten the better of King Saul and escaped the man's clutches, he still felt like he was going to be captured and harmed. David came up with the plan of escaping into the land of the Philistines, believing that if he did that, Saul would give up searching for him. David and his band of six hundred men went to a man named Achish, son of the king of Gath. When Saul heard of David's latest move, Saul did not pursue him anymore.

David stayed in the area for more than a year, during which time he went out and captured new towns. Meanwhile, the Philistines began gathering troops to do battle against the Israelites. Achish told David that he would be fighting for the Philistine army. Saul gathered the Israelite army in preparation to fight the Philistines. But he was afraid and "terror filled his heart" (1 Samuel 28:5).

Saul prayed, but the Lord did not answer him.

When the Philistines were about to attack the Israelites, they turned to Achish and told him not to let David fight with them. They were afraid that David would turn on them at the last minute. When they returned home, they found that their city had been raided. David was very sad, but he "found strength in the LORD his God" (1 Samuel 30:6). David prayed and asked God if he should pursue the raiding party, and God said yes.

David went with four hundred men to pursue the Amalekites. Two hundred men stayed behind because they were too exhausted to continue. They came across an Egyptian man who had been abandoned by his master. His master was part of the raiding party that David was trying to catch. The man agreed to show him where the party was. David caught up with them and fought them for a whole day. He recovered everything that had been plundered from his village. And he returned all of it. When the two hundred who stayed behind saw them, they were excited. But some of the four hundred men who went with David and fought did not want to share the plunder. David intervened and said they were going to share because it was the Lord who had provided, and he didn't want his people to be selfish. David sent some of the plunder to people in many towns throughout the area where he and his men had roamed.

Meanwhile, the Philistines continued to attack the Israelites and were in pursuit of Saul. Sadly, they took the life of Jonathan, who had been David's very close friend. It was a fierce battle, but soon the Philistines got to Saul and wounded him very badly. The king asked one of his own men to take his sword and use it on

Saul, but the man did not obey. "Saul took his own sword and fell on it" (1 Samuel 31:4). Once the Israelites received the news that Saul and his family were gone, they fled their towns. And the Philistines took over the land.

David heard about Saul's death when a messenger came and told him the sad news. That's

also when David learned that his dear friend Jonathan had also lost his life. David and his men tore their clothes in frustration and mourned for Saul and Jonathan. Over time, David prayed and asked God what he should do now that Saul was gone.

God told David to go to Hebron, which was a place in the land of Judah. After David and his people moved, the men of Judah came and "anointed David king over the tribe of Judah" (2 Samuel 2:4). One of Saul's other sons, Ish-Bosheth, became king over Israel and reigned for two years. David ruled for seven years as king in Hebron.

 CLUES

The kings' armies fought, but David's side won. The Bible says that David continued to grow stronger and stronger, while the house of Saul became weaker and weaker.

Becoming King

When David was thirty years old, he became king over Israel. He reigned for forty years. He continued to be successful and even won Jerusalem from his enemies because "the LORD God Almighty was with him" (2 Samuel 5:10).

David defeated the Philistines and then gathered together all the thirty thousand young

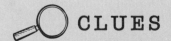

The ark of the covenant was a gold-covered wooden chest that had two angels on the cover and contained the two stone tablets of the Ten Commandments. This ark symbolized God's presence, so it was important for David that it was with him and his people in Jerusalem.

men of Israel and brought the ark of the covenant back to Jerusalem.

As time passed, David felt convicted because he didn't think it was right that the ark of God was being housed in a tent while he was living in a palace. There was a prophet named Nathan who was a good friend of David's. When David voiced his concerns, Nathan told David he should do as he pleased because the Lord was with him (2 Samuel 7:3).

David made a habit of praying to God in an act of worship. The Bible records his many victories in battle, and he was blessed in everything he did. Along the way, David had a son named Absalom.

Absalom was not a very nice person, and he set out to take over the power that had been set aside for his father. Absalom would stand by the city gate and intercept the people who had come to talk to David. He promised people justice if they would help get him appointed judge in the land. The Bible says, he "stole the hearts of the people of Israel" (2 Samuel 15:6).

David knew that the people's hearts were turning toward Absalom, so he told his officials that they had to join him in leaving Jerusalem. They went out across the valley and up the Mount of Olives. David and his people continued traveling away from his son, who was trying to take David's life.

Absalom went

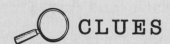 CLUES

This same thing had happened to David with Saul. David was being chased by someone close to him. He was being hunted even though he hadn't done anything wrong.

out in search of David. Meanwhile, David sent troops out to intercept Absalom, but the king told his commanders to "be gentle with the young man Absalom for my sake" (2 Samuel 18:5). A big battle took place between David and Absalom's men in the forest of Ephraim. The fighting spread out across the whole countryside.

As Absalom was riding his mule through the forest, his hair got caught on the branches of a large oak tree. The mule kept going, which caused Absalom to fall off. He was literally hanging by his hair. One of David's men found Absalom and obeyed the king's orders not to bring harm to his son. But another soldier named Joab did not obey, and he quickly found Absalom and took his life. King David eventually got the news of his son's death, and he was very sad (2 Samuel 18:33).

Eventually David returned to his palace in

Jerusalem, but things would not return to normal.
A troublemaker named Sheba didn't want David
to be king, so he started telling the men of Israel
not to have anything to do with the king. For some
reason, they listened and deserted David.

7

Final Days

For three years famine ravaged the land, and David faced even more battles with enemy lands. But each time God delivered David, and each time David learned more about just how big and mighty God is. In 2 Samuel 22:2–3, David wrote these words:

> The LORD is my rock, my fortress and

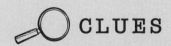

CLUES

Everything David believed had to do with God's wonderful character. At times in his life, David made bad choices, but he always wanted to make his relationship with God better. David made God his refuge, because he knew no other way. David understood that keeping a good connection to God was the best and only way to live a life that honored God.

my deliverer; my God is my rock, in whom I take refuge, my shield and the horn of my salvation. He is my stronghold, my refuge and my savior.

The Bible records the last words of David before he died. This is a small section of those final thoughts:

If my house were not right with God, surely he would not have made with me an everlasting covenant, arranged and secured in every part. (2 Samuel 23:5)

David wanted to make sure that things were right between him and God. He wanted to leave a legacy of hope for his people. Even at the end of his life, when he was very old, David had to deal with difficult situations. The Bible says that David's son

Solomon was in line to become king after David. But his other son, Adonijah, appointed himself king instead. David's wife Bathsheba came to tell the king about the problem. Even David's prophet Nathan told the king about the dilemma.

David ordered his priest and prophet to go to Solomon and anoint him the new king. Then they were told to have Solomon come back to the palace to sit on the throne as Israel's new king.

Soon after this, King David's time was near. He took his son Solomon aside and had a very powerful talk. David said, "Be strong, act like a man, and observe what the LORD your God requires: Walk in obedience to him, and keep his decrees and commands" (1 Kings 2:2–3). By the time David finished his work, he had been king over Israel for forty years.

Songs

The Psalms in the Bible are actual songs meant to be sung to the Lord in worship. The Bible names David as the author of seventy-three of the one hundred and fifty psalms. While there isn't room to look at all of them in this book, the themes mentioned in these first psalms of David are common and found in all of David's songs.

Psalm 3 is the

 CLUES

By looking at some of the psalms David created, we can get a better understanding of who God is and how David talked to Him. The psalms are encouraging and raw in honesty. They help us know that God is always in control and wants to give His children the best He has to offer. God doesn't hold back. He loves us, and His love is overwhelming!

first of the psalms written by David. David was struggling with feeling that God was somewhere else besides in his life. He cried out that his enemies were many and that God wouldn't deliver him from the fray. However, David wouldn't give in to fear and said that God was his shield, the One who lifted his head in times of trouble. David knew God heard his cries for help and that He was the One who sustained him. David wouldn't fear because he knew God loved him.

Psalm 4 is also written by David and shows how the king asked God for mercy and answered prayers. David reminded his audience that God hears us when we call to Him. He also reminded us to trust God and let our hearts be filled with His joy. God covers us with His peace and lets His face shine on us. God alone helps us to live in safety.

In Psalm 5, David asked God to hear his prayer for help. He saw the morning as the time to give all that is on your heart to God and wait on Him to move and answer according to His will. David taught that because of God's great love, we should praise Him. David wanted God to lead him in righteousness and make his way straight. David also sang about taking refuge in God and that God would protect those who love Him and that those people would rejoice. David sang that God surrounds His people like a shield.

In Psalm 6, David asked God for mercy and healing. He cried out that his soul was aching, and he wanted God to deliver him from the pain. The psalms share real emotions, and they were written to communicate a man's heart for his Creator. David called out to God and said he was worn out from groaning. David said he flooded his bed with tears and his eyes were weak from sorrow. The best part was that David knew God heard his prayers.

Psalm 7 shows David taking refuge in God. Again, David cried out to God for help in a stressful situation. David asked for justice and prayed for God to rise up and protect him. And even though David was going through difficult times, he said he would give thanks to God because God is righteous.

Psalm 8 begins with David praising God's holy and majestic name. David stood in awe of the fact that God cared for him. He sang words that remind us that God has given us His amazing grace and glory.

Psalm 9 teaches us to always be thankful for what God has given. David sang that he would tell everyone about how great God is and that he would praise His name. David wrote that his enemies turned away because of God's mighty presence. David said that God held him up. He sang of God's eternal reign. David wanted others to know that God is their refuge and a strong, safe place when trouble comes.

Psalm 11 reminds us that God is righteous and loves justice; and Psalm 12 lets us know that it is okay to call out to God for help. David said that God cares for and protects the poor from evildoers. Many of David's psalms are very emotional and show him crying out to God for reassurance. In Psalm 13, David said to God, "I trust in your unfailing love; my heart rejoices in your salvation. I will sing the LORD's praise, for he has been good to me" (vv. 5–6).

Psalm 14 shows that David wanted people to know God is reliable—He is there for us. David sang that God is our salvation and that God again is our refuge and our everything. And Psalm 15 reminds us what David knew to be important in life. He said that we need to watch how we talk to others and help our friends. We need to honor God with our behavior, even when making the right decision is hard.

Power File

Now that we've investigated the story of King David, it's time to study some lessons we can learn from his life. We will look at ten Power-Ups that will help us connect scripture to our daily lives. Memory verses go along with each Power-Up to help us plant God's truth in our hearts.

Power-Up #1:
GOD IS STRONG ENOUGH!

When David faced Goliath, he saw the giant as a problem to be solved because the enemy was going against God. David reminds us that our struggles in life belong to God. Jesus has already won the battle! We can't rely on our own strength to handle life's problems. We rely on God, because He is strong enough.

MEMORY VERSE: "It is not by sword or spear that the LORD saves; for the battle is the LORD's." 1 Samuel 17:47

Power-Up #2:

GOD LOOKS AT PEOPLE'S HEARTS. WE SHOULD TOO.

When Samuel went to Jesse in search of the next king to anoint for God, Jesse incorrectly assumed one of his older, stronger sons would be the chosen one. But we learn that God doesn't judge by outward appearances.

This is a good principle for us to practice. We have to remember that we can't know anything about a person just by looking at them.

Power-Up #3:
STAND UP FOR GOD.

David became upset when he heard Goliath talking badly about the armies of God. Since David was still very young, King Saul didn't think sending him to fight Goliath was a good idea. That's when David continued to stand up for God by showing Saul he wasn't afraid.

God had rescued David from wild animals after all. So he knew that God was certainly big enough to rescue him from the giant. We can have the same confidence as David as we face our own "giants" in life. We can have the courage to know that God is always with us!

Memory verse: "The LORD who rescued me from the paw of the lion and the paw of the bear will rescue me from the hand of this Philistine." 1 Samuel 17:37

Power-Up #4:
GOD IS WITH YOU.

After David defeated Goliath, the king invited him in to be a part of his team. Saul sent David out on missions, and David was always successful. So Saul gave David a high rank in the army. David found success in *all* the things he did because God was right there with him.

This is a great lesson to remember. God will use you to be a part of His kingdom work. Don't worry about making mistakes. God will go before you to lead the way!

Memory verse: In everything he did he had great success, because the LORD was with him. 1 Samuel 18:14

Power-Up #5:
GOD IS IN CONTROL.

David spent many of his days running away from Saul. David could have chosen to handle things differently. But he wanted to honor God, and he knew that God was in control of his life.

We can have this same attitude in our own lives too. We can step out in faith knowing that God is in charge all of our days.

Memory verse: Day after day Saul searched for him, but God did not give David into his hands. 1 Samuel 23:14

Power-Up #6:
FIND ALL YOUR
STRENGTH IN GOD.

David made sure he relied on God. For wisdom and strength, David went to his Creator for help. This is like the image of Jesus that's mentioned in the New Testament when Jesus tells the story of how one man built his house on the sand while a second man built his house on rock.

God is our rock. He is where our strength comes from. Jesus said when the storms of life come, the house built on the rock won't fall down.

Power-Up #7:
GOD IS YOUR ROCK!

Like we said in Power-up #6, God is bigger and stronger than we will ever know. When we understand that He is our rock, we know that He is unchanging.

God is our immovable foundation who will never change His mind about us. He loves you, and that's the way it will always be! Rely on God to be there for you all the time.

Memory verse: "The LORD is my rock, my fortress and my deliverer." 2 Samuel 22:2

Power-Up #8:

GOD MAKES YOUR
LIFE SECURE.

God made you, and He loves you very much. He takes every difficult day and makes things better. God is always there to look out for you. He never turns away.

David reminds us to stay connected to God and keep reading the Bible so we will always know what He wants for us. God makes your life secure so you don't have to worry about anything. He's got this!

Memory verse: Spread your protection over them, that those who love your name may rejoice in you. Psalm 5:11

Power-Up #9:

OBEY GOD AND
BE STRONG.

God is calling you to be a big part of His kingdom work. To do a good job, you must understand that God's ways are *always* best.

Obeying God will keep you connected to Him and help you follow the path He has made for you.

-

Power-Up #10:
GOD GIVES YOU REST.

Just like David wrote his songs from his experiences with God, we can also live each day knowing that God is with us. David was a shepherd, and so he came to see God as his Shepherd. We are God's children, so we can know that God is for us and wants us to have good rest.

Everything we need, God has for us. Everything we look for in life can be found in God. Let this lesson fill your heart with confidence and hope!

Collect Them All!

Kingdom Files: Who Is Jesus?
This biblically accurate biography explores the life of Jesus while drawing readers into a fascinating time and place as they learn about the One who gave sight to the blind, made the lame to walk, raised people from the dead, and who died so that we might live.

Paperback / 978-1-68322-626-0 / $4.99

Kingdom Files: Who Was Daniel?
This biblically accurate biography explores the life of Daniel while drawing readers into a fascinating time and place as they learn about the faithful man of God who interpreted dreams for the king and ultimately survived a den of hungry lions.

Paperback / 978-1-68322-627-7 / $4.99

Kingdom Files: Who Was Esther?
This biblically accurate biography explores the life of Esther while drawing readers into a fascinating time and place as they learn about the beautiful Queen of Persia who hid her Jewish heritage from the king and ultimately risked her life to save her people.

Paperback / 978-1-68322-629-1 / $4.99

Kingdom Files: Who Was Jonah?

This biblically accurate biography explores
the life of Jonah while drawing readers into a
fascinating time and place as they learn about
the reluctant prophet who said "no" to God, was
tossed overboard during a storm, and swallowed
by a giant fish.

Paperback / 978-1-68322-630-7 / $4.99

Kingdom Files: Who Was Mary, Mother of Jesus?

This biblically accurate biography explores the
life of Mary while drawing readers into a fascinating time and place as they learn about the cou-
rageous young teenager who said "yes" to God and
ultimately gave birth to the Savior of the world.

Paperback / 978-1-68322-631-4 / $4.99

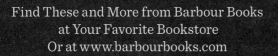

Matt Koceich is a husband,
father, and public school teacher.
He and his family live in Texas.